This Notebook
Belongs To:

____

____

live
MORE
worry
LESS

Time to head back to
Amazon to order
another book. If you
enjoyed this notebook,
we hope you will
share your opinion
by leaving a review
on Amazon.
Thank you,
Inspired Lines